Original title:
Swaying in the Tropics

Copyright © 2025 Creative Arts Management OÜ
All rights reserved.

Author: Alexander Thornton
ISBN HARDBACK: 978-1-80581-699-7
ISBN PAPERBACK: 978-1-80581-226-5
ISBN EBOOK: 978-1-80581-699-7

Ethereal Veils of the Ocean Mist

The waves wear hats of foam so grand,
Fish parade, thinking they're in a band.
Seagulls squawk their daily gossip tune,
While crabs dance beneath the crescent moon.

Jellyfish jelly on the beach we'll find,
They giggle as the tide pulls them behind.
Starfish play poker, losing will ensue,
But they don't mind—they've got nothing to lose!

Tranquil Tides and Silken Sands

A shrimp with shades thinks he's quite the star,
He struts along, showing off from afar.
Turtles lady-dance with shells on their backs,
While kids chase shadows and the sun attacks.

Coconuts fall like tiny cannonballs,
Roll like comedians through sandy halls.
Laughter and fun echo through the bay,
As waves tickle toes in a splashing ballet.

Dreaming Beneath Frond Canopies

Parrots gossip about the gossiping waves,
While monkeys play tag with the light that saves.
Leaves wave their hands, a tropical cheer,
Blowing the worries away with a sneer.

Chameleons flex in their shades of green,
Competing for laughs in this leafy scene.
Sunbeams crack jokes, shining so bright,
While lizards debate if they'll take flight tonight.

Tempting Tides in a Serene Postcard

Pineapples wear little hats of delight,
Joking with coconuts, they're quite a sight.
The waves take selfies, capturing the fun,
While clams are snapping photos under the sun.

Clouds wear sunglasses, looking so cool,
While dolphins jump through the ocean like fools.
A tropical breeze plays the jovial song,
As laughter and joy drift along all day long.

Colors of a Caribbean Dawn

The sun spills orange in a clumsy way,
A parrot squawks, 'Hey! It's time to play!'
Flip-flops dance on the wobbly pier,
While coffee spills and there's laughter near.

The sea gleams bright like a newly washed car,
A crab performs, mimicking a rock star.
Coconuts wobble, ready to drop,
As island tunes make the heart go bop.

Secrets of the Jungle Heart

Monkeys gossip in the leafy fray,
Claiming they saw a snake make a play.
Frogs sing loudly, a ribbeting band,
While the shy sloth tries to take a stand.

Vines twist like dancers, feeling quite spry,
While toucans laugh from the branches up high.
A boisterous breeze tickles all around,
With jungle whispers echoed without sound.

Twilight's Hush on Island Shores

The sun dips low, as the seagulls swoon,
Shells gossip softly beneath the moon.
A starfish grins while posing for the tide,
As playful waves come, a frothy slide.

Beach towels flutter like flags in a race,
While crabs scuttle, a comical chase.
Sandcastles wobble, wearing crowns of weeds,
As laughter rises, fulfilling beach needs.

Palms Bowed by the Sweet Zephyr

Palms do the limbo, oh what a sight,
Bending low for the breeze, feeling just right.
The coconuts giggle, they hang so high,
While the wind tells jokes as it breezes by.

Bikini-clad folks strike an awkward pose,
With sunburned noses and sand-covered toes.
A distant ukulele strums silly tunes,
While the beach bums grin, under lazy moons.

Cascades of Petals and Juicy Tropics

Palm fronds tickle the sun,
As fruit drinks tumble and run.
Laughter bursts like coconuts,
While monkeys cheer with silly struts.

The mangoes dance on the trees,
As parrots squawk with the breeze.
Tourists slip on vibrant spills,
Chasing waterfalls and cheap thrills.

Coconuts roll down the path,
While locals can't help but laugh.
With every splash and every cheer,
The world feels lighter, oh so dear!

Harboring Secrets in Vibrant Hues

The hibiscus wears a smile,
While lizards prance with style.
Frogs in shades of lime and blue,
Chorus songs that blend and stew.

Colorful shirts and sandy feet,
Wiggle dances to the beat.
Salty air tickles the nose,
As laughter jingles like windblown clothes.

In the market, fruits collide,
With jokes served up on the side.
Under umbrellas, tales unfurl,
The secret life of tropical swirl.

Twilight Blossoms and Melodic Breezes

Evening comes with a shimmer,
As stars upon the waves glimmer.
The crickets hum a catchy tune,
With fireflies dancing 'neath the moon.

Cocktail umbrellas lost in sand,
As locals stretch their sunbaked hand.
The night holds tales of mischief rife,
With laughter mapping out each life.

In twilight's grip, we sway and spin,
As themes of joy weave under the skin.
We toast to mishaps, we cheer and jest,
In vibrant realms where humor's best!

The Call of the Wild at Dusk

As shadows stretch, the day slips sly,
The alligators wink their eye.
Feet find rhythm in the jungle maze,
As critters join in the twilight phase.

The howler monkeys toss their jokes,
While night-blooming flowers take no pokes.
We stumble over tangled vines,
And share our dreams with the moon's signs.

In the whispers of the dusky air,
Laughter lingers without a care.
The wild calls out with cheeky glee,
In nature's playground, wild and free!

Dance of the Palm Fronds

Palm fronds twist and twirl,
As if they've found a pearl.
They shimmy in the breeze,
Chasing after honey bees.

Breezy limbs with flair,
Taking selfies, unaware.
They poke each other's leaves,
Swaying on their little knees.

Coconuts join the fun,
Rolling around, just for a run.
Laughing with every drop,
In this tropic, never stop.

They dance till the sunset fades,
In a concert of leafy shades.
The moon peeks with a grin,
Let the night games begin!

Whispering Waves at Dusk

Waves whisper secrets low,
Tickling toes, oh what a show!
They splash and giggle out loud,
As each boat drifts past, so proud.

Seagulls join with cheeky calls,
Joking as they dive and sprawl.
A fish jumps up, plays a prank,
Then sinks down deep with a clank.

The sun dips behind the bay,
Painting skies in wild ballet.
A crab scuttles, tries to dance,
But trips and ends his chance by chance.

All join in the evening tune,
Under a giggling, crescent moon.
The breezy giggles never end,
As the world begins to blend.

Lullabies of the Lagoon

In quiet waters, frogs croak loud,
Forming a chorus, oh so proud.
Fireflies flicker in the night,
Winking as they dance in flight.

Turtles float with sleepy eyes,
Dreaming heavy under starry skies.
Their shells are snug like a comfy bed,
While fish debate on what's been said.

Murmurs of the reeds play soft songs,
While gentle waves hum along.
The crickets chirp with glee and cheer,
Telling tales of the day, oh dear!

As slumber wraps the lagoon tight,
Every creature sleeps in delight.
While the moon watches with a grin,
It's a party that's free of sin.

Beneath the Canopy's Embrace

Leaves perk up in joyful glee,
Whispering jokes to every bee.
A parrot cackles, joins the jest,
While monkeys swing from branch to breast.

Mossy carpets beneath our feet,
In a game of hide-and-seek, so neat.
Lizards laugh, they jump and dash,
While sunlight twinkles in a flash.

Vines tangle like a giant noodle,
Offering a ride for a little poodle.
Tangled webs, spiders weave with flair,
Making hats for the snails to wear.

Beneath the green, life's a jest,
Nature crafting its very best.
In this jungle, fun's the case,
Where every creature finds its space!

Dreamscapes Beneath the Volcano's Eye

A lizard in a sunhat sips his drink,
While birds do disco on the brink.
The lava flows, but not with heat,
    It's just a party on repeat.

A banana peel creates a slide,
Down the hill where critters glide.
A frog does flips with carefree flair,
As monkeys swing without a care.

The volcano yawns, a smoky breeze,
While iguanas dance on frozen knees.
It's quite a sight, this lively show,
As nature shakes it to and fro.

With laughter echoing through the trees,
Even the shadows twist with ease.
In this wild realm of winks and grins,
The party starts as the day begins.

Harmonious Whispers of the Rainforest

A parrot sings off-key at dawn,
While howler monkeys chime along.
The trees sway gently, just for kicks,
As frogs take turns with silly tricks.

Drip-drop, the leaves play their tune,
A turtle races, oh so slow, like noon.
Mice in tuxedos dance on logs,
While ants prepare a feast for frogs.

The mist is thick, but jokes are clear,
As sloths give high-fives with good cheer.
In a world of green where giggles rain,
Nature herself can't help but feign.

Underneath the canopy's embrace,
There's laughter sprouting all over the place.
With every rustle and every twitch,
It's a comedy show, not a hitch.

Breezy Escapades Among the Palms

Palm trees wave like they just don't care,
As birds wear hats and dance in pairs.
A crab on the shore does the crab crawl,
While seashells giggle and try to stall.

Surfers tumble; oh, what a sight!
They balance and wobble, with all their might.
The beach ball bounces across the sand,
While beach umbrellas all make a stand.

The sun's a joker, hiding behind,
A cloud of laughter that's so well-timed.
In flip-flops, the locals gather 'round,
Together, they share the silliest sound.

The ocean plays games, one wave at a time,
As seashells whistle a cheeky rhyme.
Amidst the palms and sunlight beams,
Life here flows like the oddest dreams.

The Caressing Hands of Nature's Tenderness

The breeze is tickling the blooms so bright,
While critters giggle, it's pure delight.
Caterpillars practice for their ballet,
As daisies wiggle and sway away.

Clouds make faces, all fluffy and grand,
As daisies bow, creating a band.
The ants parade with tiny drums,
Marching to the beat of nature's hums.

Bubbles in puddles reflect the fun,
While frogs play leapfrog under the sun.
The whole wide world is a laugh-out-loud,
Where even the raindrops gather a crowd.

With every gust of soft caress,
The flowers dance, they couldn't care less.
In this carnival of joy so vast,
Nature's own jesters are unsurpassed.

Rhapsody Beneath the Coconut Trees

Coconuts drop with quite a thud,
One just missed a fellow's bud!
With hats askew and drinks in hand,
We dance like crabs upon the sand.

The breeze is ticklish, oh what fun,
As we chase shadows on the run.
The island's rhythm, oh so sweet,
Turns every misstep into a feat.

Mangoes fly like boomerangs,
While pelicans shout their silly clangs.
We holler loud, 'Watch out, I say!'
As laughter twirls both night and day.

Beneath the palms, we lose our way,
In this kooky tropical ballet!
With every laugh and funny fall,
We find the joy in it, after all.

The Pulse of Exotic Gardens

In jungles bright, the creatures prance,
A parrot squawks to join the dance.
With mismatched socks and beachy hats,
We giggle at the cheeky cats.

The flowers bloom in colors wild,
A bee flies past, feels like a child!
The air is thick with scent and glee,
We chase the curls of butterflies free.

With lemonade and jokes galore,
We sip and spill, we laugh some more.
A monkey swings with style and flair,
And we just sit, without a care.

In every corner, giggles sprout,
In this odd jungle, there's no doubt.
Chasing dreams and silly schemes,
Life's a burst of vibrant themes.

Nightfall's Embrace on Sandy Shores

As twilight falls, the stars align,
We stumble 'round like tipsy wine.
With sand between our joyful toes,
We're waltzing under moonlit shows.

The crabs perform their clumsy waltz,
While we collect our tiny faults.
Two left feet grow quite the fanbase,
As we trip over in this race.

The waves join in with a gentle roar,
Tickling legs as we beg for more.
With every splash, we squeal and play,
Organs parallel, we sway away.

Nightfall whispers funny grooves,
In this seaside dance, we make our moves.
With stars as friends, we twirl and spin,
Who knew that laughter could begin?

Serenity in the Shade of Giant Leaves

Beneath the leaves, the cool breeze flows,
We hide from sun, but still, it glows.
With snacks in hand and smiles so wide,
We giggle loud, no need to hide.

The iguanas strike a pose so bold,
While we chuckle at their greens and gold.
A hammock sways, a bounce or two,
Turns into the dance of me and you.

The shade's a stage for playful pranks,
We cartwheel past the ferns and tanks.
Every rustle tells a joke or two,
This jungle gym's a riot, who knew?

With laughter echoing through the trees,
We find our joy like buzzing bees.
In nature's arms, let's laugh a lot,
For here in shade, worries are forgot.

Wandering Souls Under the Palm Canopy

Under palms, the tourists dance,
With floppy hats, they take a chance.
A flip-flop's lost, they start to frown,
But laughter echoes all around.

Coconuts fall, they scream and run,
A crab joins in, it's all just fun.
With every slip, the giggles rise,
In this paradise, no room for sighs.

Sunburnt noses, a sight to see,
With sunblock lotion, they disagree.
While drinks get spilled, and splashes fly,
They cheer and shout beneath blue sky.

So toast the heat and toast the breeze,
Life's a party, bring on the cheese!
In this canopy, the spirits soar,
In wandering souls, there's always more.

A Tapestry of Flora and Fauna

Bees buzz joyfully, quite a scene,
While flowers gossip about the green.
A parrot squawks, what's all the fuss?
A lizard struts, just look at us!

The monkey swings, oh what a sight,
Dropping bananas with sheer delight.
While iguanas pose for a pic,
For this wild world, they've got the trick.

In flowers' hues, the colors blend,
Nature's laughter has no end.
A butterfly winks, just passing through,
In this jungle, there's fun for you!

With every rustle and every cheer,
The tapestry whispers, "Stay right here!"
In this land of whimsy and cheer,
Flora and fauna make fun sincere.

Subtropical Echoes in the Night

When stars twinkle in velvet skies,
The frogs croak jokes, they're quite the wise.
A firefly flickers, and what a show,
In the moonlight, shadows dance and glow.

The palm trees sway, trying to catch
All the whispers of the night's goodbatch.
While crickets tune their evening song,
Their chorus grows, loud and strong.

A turtle pokes its head around,
Saying, "Slow down, keep your feet on the ground!"
A raccoon munches on leftover pie,
In the night, sweet laughter rises high.

Through giggles and jokes that fill the air,
The subtropical rhythm, nothing can compare.
As echoes linger, revelers sway,
In this lively show, we laugh and play.

Silhouettes in the Coastal Glow

As the sunbows down, shadows flit,
Just silhouettes, dancing a bit.
With surfboards in tow, they're here for fun,
In the coastal glow, their day's begun.

A seagull steals a chip, oh cheeky!
While kids laugh loud, their faces squeaky.
A beach ball flies, a head or two,
In this sunny scene, laughter ensues.

The sunset paints all hopes and dreams,
With golden hues and ice cream streams.
So here they are, basking in cheer,
In every wave, the giggles near.

So raise your glass to skies so bright,
In silhouettes, let's dance tonight.
With every moment, let spirits grow,
In the coastal glow, we steal the show.

Soft Murmurs of the Tropical Night

In the dark, a gecko sings,
A serenade of tiny things.
A lizard's tail makes quite the show,
Dancing as if it's in a glow.

The crickets chirp their silly song,
While underfoot, a beetle throngs.
A coconut drops with a tiny thud,
As I dodge in a comical flood.

The moon is peeking through the trees,
Making shadows on the breeze.
The fireflies flicker, bright and bold,
Chasing laughter, as tales unfold.

With each rustle in the night,
I wonder where my shoes took flight.
In this wild and wacky spree,
The tropics dance, so carelessly.

Tendrils of Green Reaching for Stars

Palm fronds wave like hands in cheer,
As if they know the party's near.
A monkey swings from branch to branch,
Wearing a hat and doing a dance.

The vines giggle, they shake and sway,
Trying to steal the sun's own ray.
The flowers grin with colors bright,
Competing for attention in the night.

Frogs croak jokes with croaky glee,
While staring contests with a bee.
A chameleon changes forms to tease,
In this leafy playground, all at ease.

With stars above like sprinkles fair,
The whole scene felt light as air.
Nature's jesters in vibrant hue,
In a comedy that feels brand new.

Cascading Shadows under Lush Arches

Under canopies, shadows dart,
A retreating crab plays the part.
While nearby, a sloth moves slow,
Making a rival for the show.

The branches reach with playfulness,
As if they're sharing in the mess.
A parrot squawks in a silly tone,
Claiming the tree as its own throne.

Fronds whisper secrets, giggle and sway,
While ants march off to seize the day.
A toucan looks with a wink and grin,
His colorful beak is dressed for a win.

In this theatre, all things collide,
Where even the roots take a bumpy ride.
As laughter echoes through the leaves,
The night's embrace never deceives.

Accompaniment of Clouds and Currents

Clouds drift by like puffy ships,
Tickling the sky with whimsical tips.
Raindrops fall, a playful shower,
As we dance in the tropical hour.

With surfboards ready on the shore,
Waves invite us, beg for more.
A sea turtle floats with a wink,
Maybe it's time for a quick drink.

The wind sings melodies through the palms,
Spreading joy with breezy balms.
A sand crab burrows in the scene,
Building castles, oh so keen.

The laughter of water, a symphony pure,
While island life offers nothing obscure.
As night blankets this merry place,
Each moment, a smile on every face.

Exotic Breaths of the Wild

Parrots squawk in afeathered dance,
Coconuts roll, oh what a chance!
Lizards lounging, basking free,
Giggling at a drippy bee.

Palm trees sway, a comical sight,
A monkey stole my drink, what a fright!
Vegetables giggle in the sun,
Hoping to cook, but they just want fun.

Fishes frolic in bubbly glee,
Testing the waters, who'll be free?
Bamboo beats a silly drum,
Jellyfish jelly, oh here they come!

Colors clash like dance hall queens,
Lively antics behind the scenes.
In this wild patch, laughter rings,
Where every creature hops and sings!

Glistening Stars and Ocean's Cradle

Stars above play hide and seek,
Waves crash loud and form a streak.
Crabs wear hats, oh what a view,
While fish flash smiles, a glimmering hue.

Moonlit waters, slick as grease,
Lobsters chase, but never cease.
A dolphin dives, a splashy cheer,
Then giggles bubble up from here.

Seashells clatter in the sand,
You'd think they're in a marching band!
As tides roll in, they tap their toes,
Making music, who really knows?

With every wave, the night grows bright,
Creatures dance with sheer delight.
In this cradle, laughter flows,
A party formed where nobody knows!

Serenade of the Verdant Coast

Waves of green, a lopsided line,
Bamboo bends, it looks divine.
Kangaroos bouncing in a row,
Ducklings waddling, 'Oh, look at Joe!'

Squirrels swing with acrobatic flair,
Dropping nuts with quite a scare.
Monkeys chatter, gossip flies,
While turtles chuckle 'Oh my, my!'

Flowers bloom in a vivid spree,
Pulling faces, just wait and see.
Each petal's joke, so fresh and new,
In a garden where laughs just grew.

This coast is wild, a staged debate,
Where nature's tunes resound, sedate.
Yet in the laughter of all it's found,
Life dances sweetly, joy abounds!

Ribbons of Color in Twilight's Embrace

Sunset paints the sky in glee,
Mangoes rolling down a tree.
Frogs in tuxedos croak a song,
While crickets chirp right along.

Twilight dazzles, brings out the fun,
Fishes flirt, 'come catch me, hon!'
Chameleons change, causing a stir,
Winking at butterflies, oh what blur!

Each leaf has a story, funky and bright,
As fireflies boogie, oh what a sight!
An iguana lounges, looking so cool,
Dropping wisdom like a wise old fool.

Ribbons of shade wrap trees so tight,
The night grows deep, yet full of light.
In this whimsy, nature plays tricks,
Where joy is found in all her picks!

The Gentle Pull of Island Life

In a hammock that swings with grace,
I met a crab doing the cha-cha lace.
Coconuts dance in the salty swirl,
While parrots gossip, giving it a twirl.

Bamboo flutes play a merry tune,
As surfboards chat with the silvery moon.
Laughter echoes from the palm-fringed shore,
Who knew life could be such a playful lure?

Starfish wear shades, looking so cool,
While sea turtles swim in a six-foot pool.
I lost my flip-flop in a game of tag,
Let's see if that silly fish will drag!

So come and join this merry mirage,
Where kites and coconuts launch a barrage.
Life's a fun ride, don't take it too hard,
We'll sip on sunshine and never discard.

Satin Skirts of Wind and Ocean

The breeze wears a satin skirt, so fine,
As it pirouettes with the bright sunshine.
Fish below in tuxedos gleam,
While mermaids giggle and share their dream.

Waves waltz with shells, a clinking sound,
As jellyfish juggle, twirling around.
I tried to dance, but tripped on seaweed,
Now I'm moored, sipping coconut, indeed!

Sandcastles rise for a royal cheer,
While crabs perform their sandy leap here.
The sun drops low with a blushing grin,
As we clink our shells—let the fun begin!

In this coastal ballet with joy to unfold,
Every wave serves laughter, brave and bold.
Let's kayak with clowns or fish with flair,
Where every splash brings giggles to share!

Blossoming Jive of the Night Flora

Underneath the stars, flowers shake in delight,
As they bust a move through the warm summer night.
With petals a-twirl and colors aglow,
Their midnight groove puts the moon on show.

Fireflies blink like a wild disco ball,
As crickets chirp a tune that enthralls.
The orchids gossip with the jasmine sweet,
As the orchid party boasts dancing feet.

Anemones sway as the seafoam joins,
While blooming laughter fills the ocean's coins.
Folks on the shore do a midnight prance,
Who knew a flower could lead the dance?

With waves as the backdrop, fun's in our sphere,
A botanical bash, we hum and we cheer.
So grab a bloom, let's shake off the strife,
And join the jive of this magical life!

Heartbeats of the Coastal Realm

The beach beats like a drum, oh so grand,
With flip-flops thumping on soft golden sand.
Seagulls squawk like they're in a band,
As the tide laughs and gives us a hand.

Bubbles and giggles bubble up loud,
With crabs doing a jig, oh so proud.
Tanned feet jump to the rhythm of waves,
In this silly dance, everyone's brave!

Old surfboards lined up in a row,
Look like they're waiting for the right flow.
As the sun dips down in a splash of red,
The ocean hums tunes that we all danced.

With laughter ringing through palm tree highs,
This realm's alive with a playful surprise.
So come along, don't be shy or scared,
In the heartbeat of fun, let's be declared!

Melodies of the Island Heart

The coconut fell, oh what a sight,
A parrot squawks, with sheer delight.
The waves laugh loud, they dance and play,
While crabs copy them, in a clumsy display.

The sun wears shades, all bright and bold,
As tourists sip drinks, ice-cold and gold.
Hammocks wiggle, like they have a mind,
And bees buzz about, quite unconfined.

A fish in a hat swims up to chat,
Telling tales of the big catch that sat.
The sand tickles toes, in a playful race,
While beach balls bounce with a silly grace.

Under palm trees where the laughter flows,
A limbo contest, as the wild wind blows.
Swing to the rhythm, twirl and prance,
In this curious place, we all take a chance.

Curves of the Coastal Breeze

The wind does a twist, a charming tease,
It spins the leaves, with effortless ease.
A toucan trips, all colors and clatter,
As shells hold secrets, and probably chatter.

The sun flips pancakes upon the bay,
As locals trade stories in a goofy way.
With each playful wave, the rhythm unfolds,
While giggles escape, like little gold molds.

The tide rolls in, with a squishy surprise,
A crab in a top hat, oh my, what a guise!
Laughter erupts, as the sea throws a fit,
And umbrellas flip, what a sight to admit.

In the glow of dusk, while fireflies blink,
A dance-off erupts, without needing a wink.
With coconut crowns and leis all around,
Joy bubbles up in this twisted playground.

Tropical Nocturne in Green

The moon takes a dip, in the glistening bay,
While crickets write songs, in their quirky way.
A lizard moonwalks, all sly and sleek,
As night unfolds secrets, colorful and cheek.

The stars chirp tunes, with a wink and a grin,
As monkeys swing by, on a nocturnal spin.
Palm fronds drum softly, in rhythm divine,
While shadows join in for an odd little line.

The ocean murmurs a joke or two,
A dolphin giggles, under the hue.
As lanterns bob, like floating balloons,
The island sighs low, humming silly tunes.

In this quirky night, full of playful sights,
A party of critters dances with delights.
So grab your flip-flops, and let's take a stroll,
Through this laughter-filled, giggle-brown hole.

A Tangle of Vines and Ambiance

The vines stretch upward, a playful entrap,
While sloths roll over, in a lazily nap.
The sunbeams tilt, like a comic book line,
And parrots tell stories, well-sipped and fine.

The forest chuckles, with a rustle and tease,
Mice have a meeting beneath the tall trees.
As bananas gossip, all yellow and bright,
An iguana drums, keeping time just right.

A snake does a shimmy, in search of a snack,
While frogs hold a party, all green and whack.
In this tangled wonder, laughter will reign,
With critters all dancing in a silly chain.

With foliage swaying, a rhythm, a beat,
The creatures unite, for a hilarious feat.
So join in the fun, in this world set apart,
Where vines and laughter create the true art.

Rhythm of the Setting Sun

In the hammock, I doze and sway,
Caught between night and the light of day.
A coconut falls, bonks my head,
I laugh it off, dream of bread.

The roosters crow, they think they're cool,
While I'm dancing here like a fool.
Sandals flop with every step,
A lizard laughs—I need a rep.

The waves clap hands on the golden shore,
As crabs do a jig, wanting more.
Bright parrots gossip on a branch,
While I trip over my own pants.

As daylight dims, I drink my rum,
Imagining I'm a famous bum.
With palm trees swaying, quite a show,
Even the sun can't help but glow.

Serenade of the Sapphire Sea

The ocean hums a silly tune,
Inviting me to join real soon.
A fish jumps high, tries to sing,
I cheer it on—what a weird thing!

Mermaids giggle in the foam,
Wishing I'd just stay at home.
They brush their hair, and tease their tails,
While I'm tangled in my own gales.

The crabs compete in a clumsy race,
While I break dance, losing face.
With every splash, a giggle bursts,
I try to swim, but it's the worst.

Yet under the sun, pure glee takes flight,
In the water, everything feels right.
As the sea winks and plays nearby,
I belly flop, and simply fly.

In the Shade of Tropical Dreams

Under palm trees, I take a nap,
While a toucan steals my snack.
Woke up laughing at my fate,
As he squawks, 'C'mon, don't be late!'

Sunshine warms my squinty eyes,
While monkeys drop fruits, oh what a surprise!
I try to dodge, but I can't escape,
Bananas fly like they're in shape!

With dreams of pineapple in my head,
I wiggle around, then fall instead.
Laid back in laughter, I just can't miss,
Life's a party, sealed with a kiss.

The breeze whispers jokes just for me,
As I sway with the leaves, so carefree.
Here every jest is needed for fun,
As laughter lingers from dawn to sun.

Echoes of the Gentle Breeze

A breeze dances through the trees,
Tickling my nose, stirring the leaves.
A parrot squawks, "Get off your chair!"
While I stifle a snicker, without a care.

The sun can't stop its giggly glow,
While waves slap dance, putting on a show.
I tripped on flip-flops, fell with grace,
And higher than clouds, my spirits race.

The local goats join the choir,
Munching grass while up on a wire.
If only the dogs would sing a tune,
We'd hold a concert beneath the moon.

As shadows lengthen, we gather near,
Spinning tales filled with laughter and cheer.
In this paradise, with fun set free,
Who needs a map? Just come dance with me!

Dance of Fireflies at Dusk

A waltz of light in the air,
Little bugs without a care.
They twirl and spin, oh what a sight,
Bumping into trees, oh what a fright!

With every glow, they seem to laugh,
A midnight party, a tiny gaffe.
Caught in webs of giggling fright,
Even spiders join the flight!

Their dance continues, with all it's flair,
In neon suits, without a pair.
Who knew bugs had such great moves?
They shimmy and spin, they definitely groove!

As dusk takes hold, the stars awake,
Each little flash, a party to make.
With glow-in-the-dark, they boast so bright,
Wondering who still needs a light!

The Secrets of Sunset's Glow

Oh, the sun dips low, a mystery bright,
Painting skies in hues of might.
"What are you hiding?" the clouds inquire,
While flamingos gawk, they never tire!

A golden orb that winks and grins,
Telling tales of day's silly sins.
It blushes red; must be a crush,
While crabs collect shells in a rush!

Birds line up for a last, sweet song,
While fish swim by, thinking they belong.
"Why so shy?" the horizon chimes,
As laughter rolls like the ocean's rhymes!

With each drop of light, the giggles flow,
As night creeps in with an afterglow.
The secrets held in colors bold,
Dancing shadows, stories told.

Dancing Palms Under Moonlight

Tall and proud, the palms do sway,
But not with grace, oh what a play!
They do the twist, they do the turn,
In the moon's light, they laugh and churn!

The coconuts chuckle as they drop,
'This is the night, let's start the bop!'
With every breeze, they shimmy and quake,
Eyes wide open, make no mistake!

Laughter echoes down the lane,
As shadows dance, the vibe's insane.
Crabs can't help but join the scene,
In this moonlit waltz, so serene!

Oh what a sight, these palms at play,
Jiving and jiving till the break of day.
With every rustle, the laughter spreads,
As nature twirls on her leafy threads!

Whispering Winds of Paradise

The breeze tells tales, so soft and sly,
Of playful fish and birds that fly.
They giggle past the sandy shore,
Tickling toes, and wanting more!

"Did you hear that?" the palm trees quip,
As every gust gives a cheeky tip.
They dance around with leaf-like grace,
In a comedy show, a leafy race!

Winds swirl laughter in their embrace,
Swaying to rhythms at a cheeky pace.
The flowers laugh with colors bright,
While clouds poke fun at day and night!

"Oh what a world!" the waves declare,
"Join our party, if you dare!"
With whispers sweet, they pull you near,
As nature's jesters spread the cheer!

Radiance of Nature's Embrace

The sun's a jester, bright and bold,
It tickles leaves, or so I'm told.
Lizards laugh on stones so warm,
As butterflies pretend to swarm.

Coconuts drop with a clunk,
While monkeys dance and twist in funk.
Parrots squawk with witty grace,
Nature's stand-up, in this place.

Palm fronds wave like hands in cheer,
Inviting everyone to near.
With laughter bubbling in the breeze,
This paradise aims to please!

So join the fun, let worries melt,
In this bright land, a joy is felt.
Where nature's quirks are never shy,
In a world where giggles fly high.

Tides of Tranquility and Silence

The ocean whispers, soft and clear,
Yet somehow, it's too full of cheer.
Waves burp loudly with a splash,
While crabs scuttle with a dash.

Seagulls swoop, with styles to brag,
Stealing fries from your old bag.
As sunbeams play hide-and-seek,
I wonder who's the loudest geek.

A ship sways like a dad in dance,
While fishes giggle at romance.
The tides roll in, a tidal wave,
Leaving ships cool vibes to save.

So take a breath, relax a sec,
Let calmness spin, a funny wreck!
In waves of laughter, feel the grace,
Here's nature's own warm embrace.

Petals Drifting on the Soft Wind

Blossoms flutter down like clowns,
Catching breezes, wearing crowns.
The daisies chuckle, spilling tea,
While butterflies shout, 'Look at me!'

With petals tumbling, a wild race,
A flower parade, full of grace.
They giggle as they flutter low,
In this floral show, there's no woe.

The garden's a stage, oh what fun,
Bees buzz along, not done, not done!
And if you listen closely now,
You'll hear the flowers take a bow.

So join this bloom of giggly beats,
As nature throws her fun retreats.
In colors bright, and scents divine,
Here blooms a world that's truly fine.

Dance of Light Through the Canopy

Sunbeams play hide and seek,
Bouncing off the trunks so sleek.
The shadows giggle, making waves,
As sunlight dances, nature braves.

Lizards zoom, they cheer the chase,
While squirrels prance with goofy grace.
Branches wave like jazz hands, good,
As vines swirl in a playful hood.

In this green realm of light and glee,
Funky critters sway so free.
The roots tap dance, the leaves all nod,
Nature rocks its own little pod.

Come join the party, don't delay,
Where every moment's bright and gay.
Amongst the trees, laughter flows,
In this canopy, joy just grows!

Fluttering Colors Against the Sky

Parrots gossip loudly up high,
Their feathers a riot, oh my!
The sun's a hammock in the blue,
Where dreams take naps as breezes flew.

Balloons float by with a twist and turn,
Each bounce a laugh, a new concern.
A crab chases shadows, quite the race,
While boisterous waves sing with grace.

Palm fronds wave like hands in glee,
As tourists sip on iced green tea.
A dolphin did a silly dance,
In cliffside rocks, we took a chance.

With every gust, a new surprise,
The sky paints giggles as it flies.
A kite gets stuck in a tree, hooray!
Nature's charm keeps boredom at bay!

Embrace of the Velvet Night

Stars are winking, oh so bright,
While crickets chirp with pure delight.
A moonbeam slips on a cat's nose,
As laughter echoes, and joy glows.

Fireflies wear their tiny lights,
A disco party under the nights.
The palm trees sway with a lazy grin,
As coconut drinks help us begin.

A iguana struts in dapper style,
And all the turtles join in a while.
While shadows dance, we sing along,
To the melody of this wild throng.

Each wave brings a tingle of fun,
As crabs teach us how to run.
With warmth wrapped in the velvet air,
We chuckle freely, without a care.

Lullabies among the Tropic Blooms

Hummingbirds hum their sleepy tunes,
While monkeys trade their funny prunes.
Flowers giggle in the gentle breeze,
Winking at bees with sticky knees.

A butterfly flutters, oh so sly,
As ants march on with a battle cry.
The sun dips down with a cheeky joke,
Making umbrellas for the folks that smoke.

Mangoes tumble from the trees,
As parrots gossip, feeling the tease.
Children chase shadows through the sun,
While night gives way to the day's fun run.

Lullabies weave through fragrant air,
While lizards lounge without a care.
In this garden, laughter grows,
As joy erupts from every rose.

A Symphony of Rustling Palms

Palms twist like dancers on the shore,
As breezes play the bongo score.
Coconuts chuckle with a thud,
While squirrels flutter like fallen buds.

Bananas hang out, quite at ease,
Gossiping gossip with swarming bees.
With every gust, our hats take flight,
And giggles echo in pure delight.

Sandcastles sprout like mushrooms in pots,
While seagulls try to nab our knots.
The twilight paints the sky in cheer,
As nightfall whispers, "Fun times here!"

With harmonies of nature's tune,
We dance with shadows beneath the moon.
In this symphony, we play our part,
With laughter woven in our heart.

Tropical Hues at Dusk

In the sky, colors clash, oh what a sight,
The sun dances low, as day says goodnight.
Birds wear their sombreros, quite the affair,
While monkeys juggle coconuts, up in the air.

Lizards in shades that put стилы to shame,
Try to outshine the flamingo's fame.
Palm trees gossip, rustling their fronds,
Echoing laughter like breezes respond.

Waves tickle the shore, they're laughing too,
As crabs host a dance in the warm ocean dew.
Each splash a giggle, each foam a cheer,
What a wild party, all creatures draw near!

Stars peek through clouds, ready to play,
Dressing the night in their sparkly array.
But watch where you step, or you might just trip,
On a coconut rolling, it's quite the hip flip!

The Caress of Warm Breezes

Gentle whispers rustle through the leaves,
Tickling the cheeks like mischievous thieves.
The scent of bananas hangs in the air,
Even the parrots stop for a dare.

Sunbathing iguanas strike a bold pose,
While sloths toss jokes, they're the cleverest pros.
Coconuts giggle, roll down the hill,
As butterflies twirl with grace and great skill.

A monkey in shades drinks juice with delight,
He sips like a star under soft, golden light.
Nature's a stage where the laughter won't quit,
The tropical fun just won't seem to limit!

Evenings invite, with a nod and a grin,
Every critter knows this is where fun begins.
As dusk paints the world in shades of bright cheer,
A melody of laughter is all that you hear.

Secrets of the Verdant Canopy

Up in the branches, a squirrel takes flight,
Chasing his dreams in a dance of pure height.
The vines pull him close, then toss him away,
"It's just a game," he laughs, come what may!

Monkeys debate what's the best fruit to munch,
Arguing loudly over a juicy brunch.
Parrots sip cocktails from coconut shells,
Telling wild tales as they flash their bright bells.

Owls listen in, with wisdom to share,
While the chameleons boast of their newest glare.
A playful breeze carries secrets untold,
In this leafy haven, where legends unfold.

Giggles erupt from the underbrush tight,
As snails win the race at a leisurely height.
Every twist and turn is a whimsical ride,
In verdant heights, where the silly reside!

Vibrant Flora in the Evening Glow

Flowers in hues that spark giggles and glee,
Compete for attention, just wait and you'll see.
The petals gossip, their colors unite,
Swaying and posing in pure, joyful light.

Bees wearing hats buzz around in delight,
While the daisies kick back, feeling oh so polite.
Humidity joins in, giving a wink,
As frogs hop along, stopping just to think.

The moon peeks in, plays a soft tune,
While fireflies dance as if in a cartoon.
Each bloom is a laugh waiting here to unfurl,
In the laughter of blossoms, the evening's a whirl.

So let's raise a toast to the wild blooming scene,
Where petals weave stories, both silly and keen.
As night takes the hand of the light in a twirl,
In vibrant flora, let your giggles unfurl!

Nature's Whispers Under Celestial Bodies

In the trees, the squirrels chat,
One claims he's the best acrobat.
A banana peel flies with glee,
As birds gossip, sipping herbal tea.

Moonbeams sneak like kids at play,
Dancing on the leaves, come what may.
Crickets play a serenade,
While frogs join in—a grand parade.

Stars winking, the skies so bright,
Fireflies giggle, ignorant of fright.
The breeze tells tales of last week's race,
Where a snail lost but kept its pace.

Nature whispers with a hearty laugh,
Every creature revels in its craft.
Under the cosmos, the fun expands,
In this jolly land, all things withstands.

Paintbrushes of Nature's Canvas

Sunshine spills from the paint pot,
Splattering colors, a joyful plot.
Grass wears green, a vibrant suit,
While flowers flaunt their colors, astute.

Clouds dip low in a fluffy brush,
Painting the horizon in a rush.
A rainbow laughs, a playful arc,
While the wind twirls like a mad lark.

Trees shimmy in their leafy tints,
While bees buzz, laughing at hints.
Each gust whispers a colorful tale,
As we dance like leaves in the gale.

Creativity flows, a wild spree,
Nature's artwork, a sight to see.
With every stroke under the sun,
The world beckons, "Come join the fun!"

The Vibrancy of Earth's Palette

Daffodils don't take themselves too serious,
Joking with tulips—quite delirious.
Pansies giggle at the sun's bright glare,
As daisies prance without a care.

The ocean splashes paint on the shore,
Waves chuckling as they play, wanting more.
Seashells whisper, "We've seen it all,"
While crabs moonwalk, answering the call.

Bumblebees are buzzing ballads in flight,
Swapping tales of nectar, pure delight.
Even pebbles chuckle, laid in a row,
As laughter echoes in the ebb and flow.

Colors clash like buddies in a brawl,
But they find common ground, standing tall.
Each shade reminisces with a grin,
At the vibrant corners, where life begins.

Traces of Light on Misty Waters

Misty morn, the ducks wear shades,
Floating along in their cool parades.
A lily pads' stuck in a soft bog,
Swearing it's a fancy float like a log.

Ripples giggle, causing a splash,
As a fish jumps, turns with a dash.
Light twinkles, that playful tease,
Reflections of joy dancing with ease.

Frogs croak out dad jokes so crude,
While turtles nod, just playing it crude.
A heron pulls a ridiculous face,
Catching light with a splash, a comical race.

The sun's rays tickle the water's cheek,
Laughing and sparkling, so unique.
In this funny, bright light's embrace,
Nature smiles, leaving no trace of pace.

Breath of the Tropical Earth

In the jungle, monkeys swing,
Chasing dreams, they laugh and sing.
With a coconut as their throne,
They claim the world as their own.

Lizards bask in dappled light,
Critique the birds, their fashion fright.
A parrot joins, a sassy queen,
In colors bold, a fashion scene.

Palm trees dance, a comical sight,
With every gust, they twist with might.
The sun smiles wide, a goofy grin,
As critters jump, let the fun begin.

Nature's circus, wild and free,
Each creature plays, just wait and see.
With giggles echoing through the air,
The tropical charm, beyond compare.

Hidden Paths of Paradise

Through tangled vines, the laughter flows,
Where every step, a secret shows.
A toucan winks with a smile so wide,
As we stumble forth on this wild ride.

Fronds wave frantically, like a hand,
Letting us know we're in their land.
A chameleon plays hide and seek,
Changing colors so unique.

Pineapple hats on every head,
As we dance where the wild things tread.
The whispers of the wind proclaim,
We're all just players in this game.

So grab a friend, and lose your way,
In this paradise, let's laugh and play.
With each twist, a new surprise,
Hidden paths reveal the skies.

Melodies of the Rain-soaked Earth

Pitter-pat, the raindrops fall,
Each one plays a different call.
Splashing puddles, frogs in tow,
Sing along, it's quite the show.

Vibrant flowers sway and sway,
Throwing colors into the fray.
A snail slides by, in rainbow garb,
With a swagger, oh so sharp.

The clouds above, a playful tease,
Rolling in like a flurry of bees.
Elephants dance in muddy pools,
Proving nature's just for fools.

With every giggle, every cheer,
The tropic songs draw us near.
Here, laughter echoes through the rain,
In sweet duet, we'll stay insane.

The Fragrance of Distant Blooms

In the garden, petals glow,
A breeze brings scents we all know.
With bees competing for the prize,
A floral brawl before our eyes.

Hibiscus laughs in crimson shades,
While roses gossip in cascades.
The orchids flaunt their fancy dress,
Debating who looks best, no less.

Scented breezes dance along,
Old coconut trees join the throng.
A parakeet cracks a joke up high,
As blooms respond with a sweet sigh.

So take a whiff, oh joy, oh fun,
In this bouquet, we're all as one.
The fragrance floats, a giggling breeze,
As nature dances among the trees.

The Call of the Wild Orchid

A flower in a tutu sways,
Dancing in the sunlit rays.
With each gust, it twirls and spins,
Chasing after butterfly twins.

Bumblebees with silly grins,
Buzzing as if in a win.
They try to join the flowery race,
But trip and fall with style and grace.

Palm trees giggle in the breeze,
Whisper secrets to the leaves.
The wild orchid plays its part,
A comedy of nature's art.

Balmy Nights and Starry Skies

Underneath the moonlit glow,
Crickets form a lively show.
With fiddles made of twigs and leaves,
They play until the night deceives.

The stars wink down, they have a ball,
As fireflies write in the sprawl.
Each flicker laughs at the dark,
While owls hoot tunes to the lark.

A night of mirth without a care,
Laughter floats in the warm air.
Why do the frogs sing like a band?
Because the night is simply grand!

Horizon's Lament of the Day

The sun stretches out with a yawn,
Painting skies with hues of dawn.
Yet clouds come in, what a cheek,
To block the view, so rude and sleek.

A parrot squawks with loud lament,
Complaining on its branch, it's spent.
While lizards chase their own long tails,
Squeaking out their silly wails.

As twilight sneaks with a caper,
The horizon flickers like paper.
And laughter dances with the breeze,
A day well-spent, oh, such tease!

Spirits Roaming Through Ancient Trees

In the woods where old ghosts play,
They tell tall tales of yesterday.
With sticky updos made of moss,
Their hairstyles might just bring a loss.

Roots wriggle like they're in a dance,
Making creatures lose their chance.
While shadows giggle, keep it light,
As owls peer down, ready to fright.

The breeze whispers through the leaves,
With punchlines hidden, how it weaves.
Who knew that nature had such glee?
In the woods, they all roam free.

Moonlight on Tropical Waters

Beneath the stars, a fish jokes loud,
"Do I need a rental for this crowd?"
The moonlit waves do a waltz, you see,
As crabs in tuxedos serve coconut tea.

The dolphins dance, wearing sunhats wide,
While sharks in tuxes swim side by side.
A parrot sings, "Don't be so blue!"
"Just watch out for the seaweed stew!"

Garden of the Lost Isles

In the garden where pineapples wear pants,
A turtle limps, he's lost his chance.
"Where's the party?" he calls out in vain,
While bananas giggle and shrug in disdain.

Mangoes in top hats spin and twirl,
"Did we invite the squid?" they swirl.
All onlookers laugh, feeling quite spry,
As coconuts plot a coconut pie.

Reflections on a Coral Reef

A clownfish plays peek-a-boo with a snail,
While seahorses gossip, tails all in a trail.
"Did you hear?" one whispers, "A shrimp's gone rogue!"
As a lobster slides by in a sparkling frock.

Starfish boast of their five-point plans,
Trying to form a rock band with clams.
They strum on seaweed and sing quite off-key,
But the jellyfish float, laughing with glee.

Footprints in the Soft Embrace

Oh, the footprints left in the sandy bliss,
By crabs with their claws, it's hard to miss.
"Which way did he go?" a seagull squawks,
As the tide creeps in, making fresh walks.

A flip-flop flops, caught in a race,
From the hands of a child who's lost in space.
The sand sticks tight, it's a sticky spree,
Where laughter drowns out the salty sea.

Chasing Shadows in the Sunlight

In a game of tag with the heat,
My shadow darts, oh, it's fleet.
I trip on sand, do a silly twist,
Laughing loudly, how can I resist?

The sun is bright, my hat flies away,
I chase it down like a fool gone astray.
Bouncing like a beach ball in a rain,
Splats of laughter, it's all part of the game.

Seagulls drop all their judgment, I swear,
As I dance like a crab with two left pairs.
A flip-flop thief, oh what a ruckus,
Life is a joke, and I'm the circus.

With each step, the sand sings a tune,
Shells giggle softly, it's a funny boon.
I'm a shadow chaser, a giggling sprite,
Under this blazing sun, everything's light.

Lush Symphony of the Rainforest

In the jungle, where the creatures play,
A monkey yells, 'Hey, is that a toupee?'
Parrots gossip on their morning stroll,
Swinging through branches, they're on a roll.

The sloths are slow but full of cheer,
With a cocktail of leaves and a hearty beer.
Frogs sing opera, each croak is grand,
While insects host a buskers' band.

I joined the fun with a wig made of vine,
Danced like a dodo, it felt so divine!
The trees are grooving with their leafy sway,
In this verdant chaos, who needs ballet?

When the rain starts to fall, it's a splash zone,
Mud fights erupt, and I'm not alone.
The forest bursts forth, laughter ensues,
In this lush symphony, even vines have moves.

Tides that Kiss the Golden Sand

Oh, the waves are flirty, a playful tease,
They steal my sandals, with such whimsical ease.
I chase them down with a noisy squeal,
Tripping and splashing, it's the best kind of reel.

The tide's a mischief-maker; it likes to shout,
Every retreat is when they pout.
Shells giggle on the beach, rolling with glee,
'Come join the party; it's wild and free!'

With a bucket and spade, I dig for gold,
But all I'm finding is sand that's cold.
A crab scuttles by, giving me a wink,
In this sandy circus, I barely can think.

As the sun sets low, painting the sky,
I tip my hat and say goodbye.
But the tide pulls me in with a wink and a grin,
As if to say, 'You'll be back, my friend!'

Dancers Beneath the Coconut Canopy

Beneath the shade where coconuts sway,
I set my groove, come what may.
A parrot joins with a feathery flair,
As we twist and twirl without a care.

The breezes chuckle at my funny moves,
Grasshoppers join with their endless grooves.
A lizard does a solo, bold and bright,
While I trip over roots, what a sight!

The palms sway gently, cheering me on,
So I'll dance till dusk and greet the dawn.
With coconuts rolling like balls on parade,
It's a hodgepodge of fun, this jam we've made.

As laughter echoes through rustling leaves,
I'm the dancing fool the forest believes.
In this tropical ruckus, life's a feast,
With every turn, I'm the joking beast.

www.ingramcontent.com/pod-product-compliance
Lightning Source LLC
Chambersburg PA
CBHW072129070526
44585CB00016B/1599